MEMORIAL DAY

A TRUE BOOK®

by
Christin Ditchfield

Children's Press®
A Division of Scholastic Inc.

New York Toronto London Auckland Sydney
Mexico City New Delhi Hong Kong
Danbury, Connecticut

A visitor at the Vietnam
Veterans Memorial in
Olympia, Washington

Reading Consultant
Nanci R. Vargus, Ed.D.
Assistant Professor
Literacy Education
University of Indianapolis
Indianapolis, IN

Library of Congress Cataloging-in-Publication Data

Ditchfield, Christin.
    Memorial Day / by Christin Ditchfield.
        p. cm.—(A true book)
    Includes bibliographical references (p.) and index.
Contents: A very special holiday — How it all got started — America at
war — To protect and serve — A day of remembrance.
ISBN 0-516-22783-1 (lib. bdg.)   0-516-27821-5 (pbk.)
1. Memorial Day—Juvenile literature. [1. Memorial Day. 2. Holidays.]
I. Title. II. Series.
E642.D58 2003
394.262—dc21

                                                          2003004532

1 2 3 4 5 6 7 8 9 10 R 12 11 10 09 08 07 06 05 04 03

Contents

A family visiting the grave of a loved one on Memorial Day

A Very Special Holiday

On the last Monday in May, people in the United States celebrate Memorial Day. A memorial is something that is done to help remember someone who has died. Memorial Day honors all the American soldiers who died in wars. These brave men and women fought to keep the nation strong and free. They gave their lives to defend their country.

On Memorial Day, Americans show that they are grateful for this **sacrifice**. Schools, banks, and businesses close for the day. People

People watching a Memorial Day parade

People attending a
Memorial Day service

wave American flags and sing
patriotic songs. They march in
parades and attend memorial services to honor the dead. Other
holiday celebrations may be fun
and exciting. Memorial Day is a
more serious and solemn occasion.

How It Got Started

In 1861, the northern and southern parts of the United States went to war with each other. People from the northern states could not agree with those in the southern states. They argued over whether or not **slavery** should be legal. They argued about whether or

The Civil War took more American lives than any other war.

not each state had the right to make its own laws and whether states can pass laws that disagree with the U.S. **Constitution**.

These arguments led to the bloodiest war in American history. It lasted four long years. Those years were filled with misery and suffering. Families were divided. Friendships were destroyed. More than 600,000 soldiers lost their lives. Never have so many Americans died in a single war.

In the years after the Civil War, people looked for ways to remember those who had died. Some wrote poems and songs about the war heroes. Others

wore ribbons or flowers as symbols of **mourning**. Across the country, communities set aside different days to honor their dead. They decorated the soldiers' graves with flowers, wreaths, or flags. They called the new holiday "Decoration Day" or "A Day of Remembrance."

General John A. Logan had fought in the Civil War. Later, he became a senator in the United States **Congress**. On May 5, 1868, Logan made a special announcement: "The 30th of May, 1868, is desig-nated for the purpose of strewing with flowers, or otherwise decorating the graves of comrades who died

Senator
John A. Logan

in defense of their country
during the late rebellion, and
whose bodies now lie in almost
every city, village, and hamlet
churchyard in the land. . . ."

This Memorial Day ceremony in 1929 honored American soldiers who died and were buried in France during World War I.

Although thousands of people celebrated Memorial Day, it would not become an official holiday for more than a hundred years. In 1971, Congress voted to make Memorial Day a national holiday, "to be celebrated on the last Monday in May."

Memorial Day began as a way to remember those who died in the Civil War. But ever since World War I (1914-1918), people have set aside Memorial Day to honor those who have died in all American wars.

Poppy Day

During World War I, thousands of soldiers died on the battlefields of Europe. Later, poppies grew all over the fields. The bright red flowers reminded people of the blood of the soldiers. Poppies became a symbol of death in war.

In 1915, Moina Michael decided to wear a red poppy on Memorial Day to honor Americans who died in war. She convinced her friends and neighbors to do the same. People have been wearing red poppies on Memorial Day ever since.

This photo from the 1920s shows volunteers preparing to send people artificial poppies to honor soldiers who died in World War I.

The United States at War

The United States of America became a country when it won the Revolutionary War against England in 1783. Since then, the nation has taken part in many other wars. Some of these wars were fought for control of land in North America. The United States,

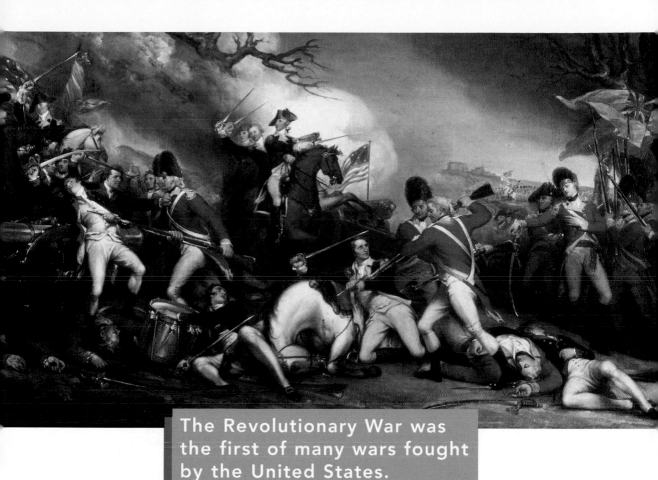

The Revolutionary War was the first of many wars fought by the United States.

Great Britain, France, Spain, and Mexico all claimed different parts of the continent as their own. They fought wars against each other, either to protect their own lands or take over someone else's. These wars included the War of 1812, the Mexican War (1846-1848) and the Spanish-American War (1898).

In World War I and World War II, most of the fighting took place in Europe and Asia. Both times, a European country started a war against another European country. Other countries joined the fight. Most of

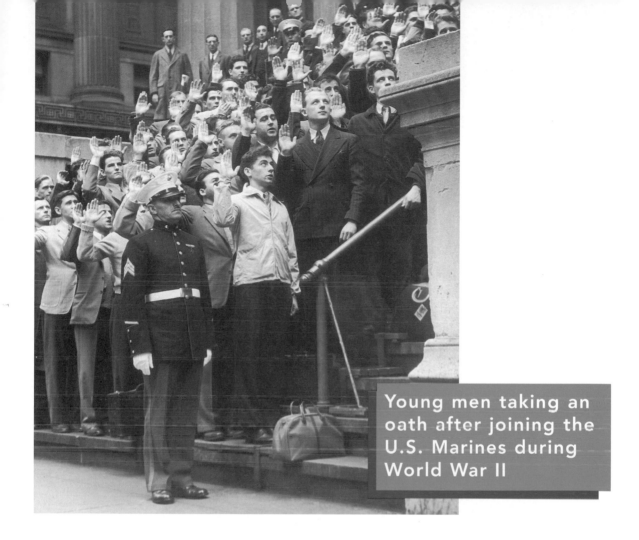

the world took sides with one country or the other. In both world wars, the United States came to the

The United States and France were allies during World War II. In 1944, French people cheered U.S. troops who had arrived to free the city of Paris from German control.

aid of its friends and **allies**. The nation understood the importance of protecting freedom around the world.

By the mid-1900s, the United States had become one of the most powerful countries in the world. Whenever its allies called for help, the country responded. Several times,

United States Army troops in Korea in 1950

American soldiers fought to prevent the spread of communism. Communism is a way of organizing a country so that all the land, houses, and businesses belong to the government.

People who live in communist countries have very little freedom. The government controls everything. Often, the governments of communist countries have tried to take over other countries and force them to become communist too. The

The Vietnam Women's Memorial in Washington, D.C., honors the American women who served in the Vietnam War.

United States tried to keep this from happening in the Korean War (1950-1953) and the Vietnam War (1954-1975).

American troops have often gone to other countries to help them. They try to keep things peaceful and safe. They try to help protect nations or governments that aren't strong enough to protect themselves. They try to prevent wars from starting in the first place.

In 1990, Iraq attacked Kuwait, a much smaller neigh-boring country. The United States helped Kuwait remain free during the Persian Gulf War.

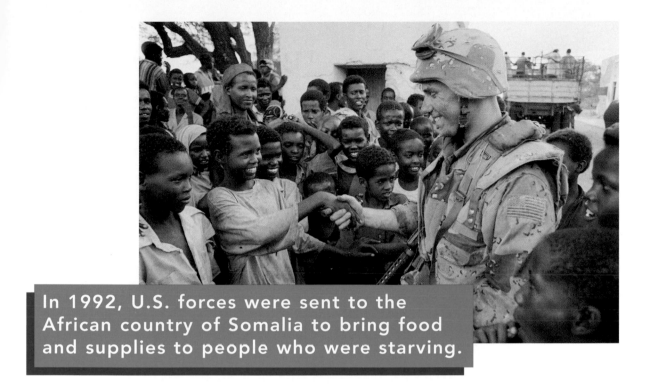

In 1992, U.S. forces were sent to the African country of Somalia to bring food and supplies to people who were starving.

After the terrorist attacks on the United States on September 11, 2001, the nation began a new kind of war—a war on **terrorism**. As President George W. Bush explained, the enemy is not one country or one political system.

In 2001, American troops were sent to Afghanistan to try to find those who were responsible for the September 11 terrorist attacks on the United States.

The United States' enemy is anyone who commits acts of violence in an attempt to destroy the lives of innocent people. In 2003, the United States and its allies began "Operation Iraqi Freedom" to stop Iraq's leaders from aiding future terrorist attacks.

"To Protect and Serve"

People in the military are often called "servicemen and servicewomen." These titles cover all of the four thousand different jobs that people have in the armed forces. Not everyone is trained in combat fighting. Some organize transportation and supplies. Some

A U.S. military radar tracker (top left), physician (top right), communications specialist (bottom left) and technician (above)

provide medical care to the sick and wounded. Others gather important information and pass it along to those who need it. Still others work as engineers, educators, office assistants, and computer experts.

The United States military has five branches: the army, navy, air force, marines, and coast guard. Each branch has its own responsibilities. Army troops are trained to fight on land, while navy troops patrol the sea. Air-force pilots attack and defend from the sky. Marines are prepared to fight on both land and sea. The coast guard protects the nation's shore and rescues ships in distress.

There are more than two million men and women on active duty in the armed forces today. In peacetime they train for war—with the hope that maintaining a strong military

(From top to bottom) The army, navy, air force, and coast guard are among the branches of the U.S. military.

U.S. marines in training

may make other countries
want to avoid starting a war in
the first place. They conduct
search-and-rescue operations.

They provide assistance to victims of natural disasters, such as floods, fires, and earthquakes. During national emergencies, they are in charge of security.

National Guard soldiers rescuing victims of a flood

Servicemen and servicewomen make many sacrifices. They may be sent anywhere in the world. At times they may have to work far away from friends and family. They know they may be called upon to give their lives for their country at any time.

The Tomb of the Unknowns

Sometimes soldiers who die on the battlefield can't be identified. No one knows who they were, but they deserve to be honored for their bravery and sacrifice. At Arlington National Cemetery, there is a special **monument** called the Tomb of the Unknowns. The **tomb** holds the remains of an unknown soldier from World War I, a soldier from World War II, one from the Korean War, and one from the Vietnam War. They represent all soldiers, known and unknown, who gave their lives for their country.

A Day of Remembrance

In all, more than one million American soldiers have been killed on the battlefields of war. On Memorial Day, Americans remember these brave men and women who died in service of their country. Many people visit war memorials and monuments in

Visitors at the Vietnam Veterans Memorial in Washington, D.C.

the nation's capital city, Washington, D.C. Each year, more than five thousand people

President George W. Bush placing a
wreath at the Tomb of the Unknowns

gather for a special memorial service at the Arlington National Cemetery. The president or vice president of the United States usually makes a speech about the bravery and sacrifice of America's soldiers. A wreath is placed at the Tomb of the Unknowns.

Around the nation, people attend similar prayer services in their own communities. Flags fly at half-mast on government buildings. Veterans

Veterans marching in a Memorial Day parade

march in parades to honor their fallen comrades. Boy Scouts, Girl Scouts, and members of other civic groups visit cemeteries to decorate soldiers' graves.

Memorial Day is the United States' promise that it will never forget the men and women who gave their lives to protect the country's freedom.

Brownies placing flags on the graves of American soldiers

To Find Out More

Here are some additional resources to help you learn more about Memorial Day:

 **Books**

Ansary, Mir Tamim. **Memorial Day.** Heinemann Library, 1998.

Bennett, William J. **The Children's Book of America.** Simon & Schuster, 1998.

Frost, Helen. **Memorial Day.** Capstone Press, 2000.

Raatma, Lucia, and Madonna A. Murphy. **Patriotism.** Capstone Press, 2000.

Sorensen, Lynda. **Memorial Day.** Rourke Press, Inc., 1994.

Stein, Richard Conrad. **Arlington National Cemetery.** Children's Press, 1996.

Organizations and Online Sites

Arlington National Cemetery
Arlington, VA 22211
http://www.arlington cemetery.org

This is the website of the nation's historic military burial ground in Arlington, Virginia.

General John A. Logan Museum
1613 Edith Street
Murphysboro, IL 62966
http://www.logan museum.org

This museum is dedicated to the Civil War veteran who founded Memorial Day in 1868.

The History Channel
http://www.history channel.com/exhibits/ memorial

This site includes photos and exhibits celebrating Memorial Day, as well as a time line of American wars, a list of related links, and resources for veterans and their families.

Memorial Day
http://www. usmemorialday.org

This site includes detailed information on the history of Memorial Day, as well as related poetry, speeches, photos, links, and tips on how to observe this special holiday.

Important Words

allies people or countries that give support to one another

Congress group of elected representatives that makes laws for the United States

Constitution document that explains the rules for the American system of government and lists the rights of all American citizens

monument something built to remind people of an important person or event

mourning act of expressing sadness and grief for someone who has died

patriotic expressing love for one's country

sacrifice giving up something for the sake of something else

slavery system in which someone is owned by another person and treated as property

terrorism using threats and violence to frighten people into obeying one's wishes

tomb grave, room, or building that holds a dead body

46

Index

Meet the Author

Christin Ditchfield is an author and conference speaker, and is host of the nationally syndicated radio program *Take It To Heart!* Her articles have been featured in magazines all over the world. A former elementary-school teacher, Christin has written more than twenty books for children on a wide range of topics, including sports, science, and history. She makes her home in Sarasota, Florida.